14
Scriptural Principles for Daily Living Vol. 5

14 Scriptural Principles for Daily Living Vol. 5

> "Your words are a flashlight to light the path ahead of me and keep me from stumbling."
> [Psalm 119:105 TLB]

Anthony Adefarakan

GLOEM, CANADA

CONTENTS

Dedication	1
Acknowledgement	2
Introduction	4
Principle #1 The Strong Tower	7
Principle #2 Weak Faith – Weak Results	11
Principle #3 He Has Forgotten	15

CONTENTS

Principle #4	A Woman - Not a Girl	18
Principle #5	How Drunk Are You?	24
Principle #6	The Vine Connection	28
Principle #7	The Bondage of Religion	31
Principle #8	Avoid the Sense Realm	35
Principle #9	The ONLY Way	39
Principle #10	All Power – Not Some	43
Principle #11	He Loves You Notwithstanding	46

CONTENTS

Principle #12 | Peace by Knowledge 49

Principle #13 | God will Make a Way 52

Principle #14 | Who Are Your Friends? 56

| Conclusion 60

| WHY YOU REALLY NEED JESUS! 61

| PRAYER POINTS 66

| BECOME A FINANCIAL PARTNER WITH JESUS 67

| About the Author 70

| 73

Dedication

I dedicate this book to God Almighty for His goodness and faithfulness in making His Word available to me. All glory to His Holy Name.

Also to everyone desirous of a closer walk with God, living out His precepts on a daily basis, I am in agreement with you all and I decree that grace for a closer walk with God is coming upon you in Jesus' Name.

Acknowledgement

I sincerely acknowledge my Eternal Father, Who alone is the Source of all wisdom. He is the Author and Finisher of my faith and it is of His fullness that the contents of this book have been drawn.

Also, I want to profoundly appreciate my dear parents – Prince and Mrs. Timothy Adefarakan – for bringing me up in the way of the Lord and for instilling righteousness consciousness in me. The wonderful education foundation I was given, coupled with their constant encouragement has empowered me to reach heights that were once beyond my imagination.

My most special appreciation goes to my sweetheart, Abisolami; without her help and support, I would never have enjoyed the conducive atmosphere needed to publish this book. I appreciate your love, encouragement, and the support you give at all times. Thank you so much. I love you, my Baby!

And to all my mentors in Ministry, I appreciate you all. Your investments in my life are not in vain. May the Lord reward you all in Jesus' Name.

Introduction

Life on earth has been described as a form of pilgrimage with eternity as man's final destination.

1 Peter 2:11 TLB says:
"Dear brothers, you are only visitors here. Since your real home is in heaven, I beg you to keep away from the evil pleasures of this world; they are not for you, for they fight against your very souls."

And Hebrews 11:13 also says:
"These men of faith I have mentioned died without ever receiving all that God had promised them; but they saw it all awaiting them on ahead and were glad, for they agreed that this earth was not their real home but that they were just strangers visiting down here."

In the course of this brief earthly sojourn, we

are bound to face certain situations capable of generating questions like *'what step do I take?' 'where do I settle?' 'who do I marry?' 'will I be rich or poor?' 'how do I finance my projects?' 'how do I take good care of my family?' 'how do I know God's will for my life?'* just to mention a few. Usually, we find it difficult to provide correct answers to these questions due to our weak mortal nature.

However, there is a manual for this pilgrimage, which is the Word of God. The One Who designed this journey for us has put in the manual all we need to navigate our way successfully and to eventually end up on the glorious side of eternity when the pilgrimage is over. Little wonder David prayed in Psalm 119:19 – *"I am a stranger in the earth; hide not thy commandment from me"*.

The principles presented in this Volume 5 are all Bible-based and will deliver results every time they are applied because the Word of God is forever settled in Heaven (Psalm 119:89).

I pray as you read on, God's grace to apply these principles will rest upon you in Jesus' Name.

Anthony Adefarakan.

Principle #1

The Strong Tower

Proverbs 18:10 KJV says *"The name of the LORD is a strong tower: the righteous runneth into it, and is safe."*

Note that it says the 'righteous runneth into it' and not the 'unrighteous'. To enjoy the safety Jesus provides, you will have to surrender your life to Him. It is when you allow Him to be Lord and Saviour over your life that you can become righteous according to 2 Corinthians 5:21.

A strong tower refers to a sure place of refuge where no harm can befall you. It's like saying *'he who dwells in the secret place of the Most High shall abide under the shadow of the Almighty'* (Psalm

91:1). It is the place of Highest Security in heaven, on earth, and beneath the earth.

Look at verses 2-10 of that Psalm 91 from King James Version: *'I will say of the LORD, He is my refuge and my fortress: my God; in him will I trust. Surely he shall deliver thee from the snare of the fowler, and from the noisome pestilence. He shall cover thee with his feathers, and under his wings shalt thou trust: his truth shall be thy shield and buckler. Thou shalt not be afraid for the terror by night; nor for the arrow that flieth by day; Nor for the pestilence that walketh in darkness; nor for the destruction that wasteth at noonday. A thousand shall fall at thy side, and ten thousand at thy right hand; but it shall not come nigh thee. Only with thine eyes shalt thou behold and see the reward of the wicked. Because thou hast made the LORD, which is my refuge, even the most High, thy habitation; There shall no evil befall thee, neither shall any plague come nigh thy dwelling.'*

All these just because you have made the Name of the Lord your refuge.

Now, what's in that Name? What makes the Name of Jesus a strong tower (place of refuge)? The answer is very simple, and it is in Philippians 2:9-11 KJV which says *'Wherefore God also hath highly exalted him, and given him a name which is above every name: That at the name of Jesus every knee should bow, of things in heaven, and things in earth, and things under the earth; And that every tongue should confess that Jesus Christ is Lord, to the glory of God the Father.'*

The Name of the Lord is the most powerful Name in the past, present, and future. It is the most respected Name in heaven and on earth. So when a righteous person engages the power in that Name, safety is secured and divine intervention is activated (John 14:14).

Are you aware of your 'righteousness' nature (as purchased for you through the shed blood of Jesus)? If yes, start using the Name of Jesus Christ actively. You have been given the authority (Mark 16:17-18).

ANTHONY ADEFARAKAN

Principle #2

Weak Faith – Weak Results

Romans 4:17-21 KJV says *"(As it is written, I have made thee a father of many nations,) before him whom he believed, even God, who quickeneth the dead, and calleth those things which be not as though they were. Who against hope believed in hope, that he might become the father of many nations; according to that which was spoken, So shall thy seed be. And being not weak in faith, he considered not his own body now dead, when he was about an hundred years old, neither yet the deadness of Sara's womb: He staggered not at the promise of God through unbelief; but was strong in faith, giving glory to God; And being fully persuaded that, what he had promised, he was able also to perform."*

The word 'weak' according to a dictionary implies lacking the power to perform...lacking physical strength and energy. It also means liable to break or give way under pressure; easily damaged.

Now, if you consider weak faith in light of those definitions, it means weak faith lacks the power to perform, it lacks strength and energy, it is liable to break or give way under pressure and it is easily damaged. That's not the kind of faith you want to run your life on.

Weak faith cannot produce desirable results. Even if it does produce any results at all, they will be weak results. In the same way you can't get a car running on a weak battery, you can't get your life running as expected on weak faith. It is better to not have any faith at all than to have a weak faith because it can be so draining and frustrating to keep thinking you are operating in faith when all the results you are getting are nothing to write home about.

One of those definitions says it is liable to break or give way under pressure, and is easily damaged. That means weak faith is not reliable. It can break under pressure. For instance, if there is a particular promise you are waiting on God to fulfill, and it is not coming to pass at the time you expect, and you give up or stop believing, it simply means what you have is a weak faith. It breaks under pressure (of delay). And the main reason weak faith breaks under pressure is because it always considers present situations. It is easily affected by what can be seen, so it is happy when things are looking good but sad when things are looking bad.

However, strong faith isn't like that. As a matter of fact, it is the opposite of everything weak faith stands for. It doesn't break under pressure, it is persistent, it doesn't pay attention to what is happening or can be seen, it is not easily damaged and as a result, has the power to perform because it is fully charged with supernatural strength and energy.

So while weak faith considers present situations

and packs up, strong faith gives glory to God for its expectations and enjoys manifestations.

That's the kind of faith Abraham exhibited when he patiently waited for the child the Lord promised him for twenty-five (25) good years. His body was dead, being 100 years old and his wife's womb was completely dead, being 90 years old (present conditions); yet he hoped against hope by not considering the deadness of his body and that of his wife but was strong in faith, giving glory to God. And what happened next? Sarah conceived and gave Abraham a son (Isaac) in his old age. Strong faith always delivers results regardless of evident contrary factors.

Principle #3

He Has Forgotten

Isaiah 43:25 KJV says *"I, even I, am he that blotteth out thy transgressions for mine own sake, and will not remember thy sins."*

Being born again means your sins have been forgiven and forgotten. When you surrender your life to Jesus Christ, there is an exchange. Your sins are transferred to Jesus (which He already paid for at the cross), and His righteousness (which He already purchased for you by His Blood) is transferred to you. 2 Corinthians 5:21 KJV says it this way: *'For he hath made him to be sin for us, who knew no sin; that we might be made the righteousness of God in him.'*

Now, the moment that exchange happens, 2

Corinthians 5:17 becomes activated in your life. King James Version renders it this way: *'Therefore if any man be in Christ, he is a new creature: old things are passed away; behold, all things are become new.'*

That means God no longer sees you as a sinner. All He now sees is another person who looks exactly like His precious sinless Son - Jesus Christ. He sees you as righteous. He can't even remember you once sinned because He has blotted them away and completely forgotten about them.

With this knowledge, you need to stop confessing what God has forgotten. If He doesn't remember, you shouldn't either. You are in His Presence for instance, about to pray, and the first words coming out of your mouth are confessions of some sins you committed a long time ago before you became saved. That's not correct. Just because you still feel bad about it doesn't mean it hasn't been blotted out. If at salvation you already asked the Lord for forgiveness and asked Him to become your Lord and Saviour, those sins are gone. The

Bible says old things have passed away, behold all things have become new. You need to understand that. What matters now is how you are going to live your life as a child of God going forward. He has forgotten and you shouldn't be reminding Him. Soak your heart with the Word of God and commence your new life on a new note.

Having said that, if you still feel really guilty about something you did wrong in the past before you became born again and it just seems not to be going away, kindly locate a mature Christian around you for some spiritual counseling. Maybe there are some restitutions you need to make for that guilt to clear off. They will be able to guide you under the influence of the Holy Spirit on what to do. And as you do whatever the Lord may be leading you to do, your peace shall be totally restored in Jesus' Name.

Principle #4

A Woman - Not a Girl

Genesis 2:18, 21-22 KJV says *"And the LORD God said, It is not good that the man should be alone; I will make him an help meet for him...And the LORD God caused a deep sleep to fall upon Adam, and he slept: and he took one of his ribs, and closed up the flesh instead thereof; And the rib, which the LORD God had taken from man, made he a woman, and brought her unto the man."*

When God was going to solve the problem of loneliness for Adam, He gave him a woman; not a girl.

If you are praying for marital settlement but you are still a girl-friend to somebody, you are not yet ready. God doesn't give away girls in marriage,

He gives away women. You must become a 'woman' by taking full responsibility on the use of your body as well as your mental faculty if you are interested in God's kind of marriage. There are things in marriage that only women can handle. If girls become exposed to such things, they will crash. For instance, virtues such as patience, humility, submission, controlled speeches, self-denial, man-handling skills among other marriage skills are not what girls can easily understand let alone exercise. If all you expect in marriage is endless fun, you are still a girl, and I strongly suggest you grow up to become a woman before you approach it.

Look at what the Bible says about a Virtuous Woman in Proverbs 31:10-31 KJV; *"Who can find a virtuous woman? for her price is far above rubies. The heart of her husband doth safely trust in her, so that he shall have no need of spoil.*

She will do him good and not evil all the days of her life. She seeketh wool, and flax, and worketh willingly with her hands. She is like the merchants' ships; she bringeth her food from afar. She riseth also while it is yet night, and giveth meat to her house-

hold, and a portion to her maidens. She considereth a field, and buyeth it: with the fruit of her hands she planteth a vineyard.

She girdeth her loins with strength, and strengtheneth her arms. She perceiveth that her merchandise is good: her candle goeth not out by night. She layeth her hands to the spindle, and her hands hold the distaff. She stretcheth out her hand to the poor; yea, she reacheth forth her hands to the needy.

She is not afraid of the snow for her household: for all her household are clothed with scarlet. She maketh herself coverings of tapestry; her clothing is silk and purple. Her husband is known in the gates, when he sitteth among the elders of the land.

She maketh fine linen, and selleth it; and delivereth girdles unto the merchant. Strength and honour are her clothing; and she shall rejoice in time to come. She openeth her mouth with wisdom; and in her tongue is the law of kindness. She looketh well to the ways of her household, and eateth not the bread of idleness.

Her children arise up, and call her blessed; her husband also, and he praiseth her. Many daughters have done virtuously, but thou excellest them all.

Favour is deceitful, and beauty is vain: but a woman that feareth the LORD, she shall be praised. Give her of the fruit of her hands; and let her own works praise her in the gates."

Those are qualities that can make you a qualified help-meet for someone. To not be virtuous is to become a liability, and no one wants to have anything to do with liabilities.

Have you ever considered what the first part of Proverbs 18:22 NKJV really means? It says *"He who finds a wife finds a good thing…"*

Did you know it means until you become a wife, you may never be found? You keep praying, worrying, and murmuring that you are of marriageable age but no man is showing interest in marrying you. In fact, what some of them want is just to have fun with you briefly and go their way, no commitment whatsoever. If this has been the case with you, it may be that you are not yet a 'wife'. Maybe you are still a girl in your thinking and attitude. You will have to become a wife material if you must be found by your own God-ordained man.

The Word of God says men are to find wives, not girls. So the moment you become a wife in your thinking, carriage, and attitude, you are close to being found. Work on yourself and stop being a girl.

Now, on the other hand, God has no plan to solve any loneliness problems for boys. He only has such plans for men. So if you are still someone's boyfriend, you are not ready for marriage.

Also, if all you do is go out with girls, you are not yet a man. To be a man you must be responsible. God didn't hand the Garden of Eden over to a boy, He gave it to Adam and made him responsible for it. And when He was going to form Eve for Adam, He said it is not good for the man (not the boy) to be alone.

So if you think having 25 or more girl-friends will solve your loneliness problem, you are joking.

It will not. In fact, doing that may even increase the vacuum in your heart and create a greater sense of loneliness in you. To be free from the loneliness God was talking about in Genesis 2:18, you need a wife. A woman; not girls. A woman; not another man. A woman; not pets. A woman; not pornography. A woman; not masturbation. That's God's order! And failure to follow this order is an inevitable invitation to persistent loneliness, chaos, depression, and if not well managed, suicide. Do some thinking about this!

Principle #5

How Drunk Are You?

Ephesians 5:18-21 KJV says *"And be not drunk with wine, wherein is excess; but be filled with the Spirit; Speaking to yourselves in psalms and hymns and spiritual songs, singing and making melody in your heart to the Lord; Giving thanks always for all things unto God and the Father in the name of our Lord Jesus Christ; Submitting yourselves one to another in the fear of God."*

According to a dictionary, to be drunk is to be affected by alcohol to the extent of losing control of one's faculties or behavior.

A drunk can be recognised at a glance, and so should a Spirit-filled Christian. If you have to wear suits or tie scarfs before you are recognized as a

Holy Ghost filled Christian, you need to revisit the 'Upper Room' – Acts 2:1-15.

When you are filled with the Holy Spirit, He starts speaking through you, and you literally begin to operate under His influence. Certain things begin to happen in your life. For instance, you start bearing the fruit recorded in Galatians 5:22-23 KJV *'...the fruit of the Spirit is love, joy, peace, longsuffering, gentleness, goodness, faith, Meekness, temperance: against such there is no law.'*

Things that used to get you upset before no longer makes you mad; you suddenly begin to exercise more patience with people, loving them for who they are and even going all the way to be good to them. Before you know it, those around you will begin to notice you are no longer the same person they used to know. That means the 'drunkenness' is beginning to show. Then you move past that and begin to operate spiritual manifestations (gifts of the Spirit) as recorded in 1 Corinthians 12:1-11 KJV *'...Now there are diversities of gifts, but the same Spirit. And there are differences of adminis-*

trations, but the same Lord. And there are diversities of operations, but it is the same God which worketh all in all. But the manifestation of the Spirit is given to every man to profit withal. For to one is given by the Spirit the word of wisdom; to another the word of knowledge by the same Spirit; To another faith by the same Spirit; to another the gifts of healing by the same Spirit; To another the working of miracles; to another prophecy; to another discerning of spirits; to another divers kinds of tongues; to another the interpretation of tongues: But all these worketh that one and the selfsame Spirit, dividing to every man severally as he will.'

Did you see that? You suddenly begin to know things in the Spirit without anyone telling you in the natural realm; you begin to prophesy and perform miracles by the power of the Holy Spirit. Now, at this point, the 'drunkenness' can no longer be hidden. The rivers of living water begin to flow through you and God's purposes begin to find fulfillment through the power of God at work in you. You no longer speak ordinary words as your words now carry power.

Even after this level, there are still higher levels of 'drunkenness' as you keep walking with God in spirit and in truth, speaking in psalms and hymns and spiritual songs, singing and making melody in your heart to the Lord, giving thanks always for all things unto God and the Father in the name of our Lord Jesus Christ, etc.

So look at your life as a believer; how drunk are you?

Principle #6

The Vine Connection

John 15:1-6 KJV says *"I am the true vine, and my Father is the husbandman. Every branch in me that beareth not fruit he taketh away: and every branch that beareth fruit, he purgeth it, that it may bring forth more fruit. Now ye are clean through the word which I have spoken unto you. Abide in me, and I in you. As the branch cannot bear fruit of itself, except it abide in the vine; no more can ye, except ye abide in me. I am the vine, ye are the branches: He that abideth in me, and I in him, the same bringeth forth much fruit: for without me ye can do nothing. If a man abide not in me, he is cast forth as a branch, and is withered; and men gather them, and cast them into the fire, and they are burned."*

Experiencing divine healing is inferior to living in divine health. The former involves getting sick and recovering supernaturally without the aid of medications or the likes while the latter implies not even falling sick at all regardless of the pathogens (disease-causing organisms) around. Both are good, but one is surely better.

Now let's look at our text carefully. Jesus said He is the true vine and His followers (including us) are the branches (connected to Him). Meaning the only way the branches can draw nourishment and thrive is if they remain connected to the vine. Right? So if any branch disconnects, it dies; that's easy to understand because He already said in verse 5 that without Him we can do nothing. That part is clear enough.

But think about this, if all branches get their nourishment or supplies from the vine, it does mean that whatever is flowing in the vine is what flows into them. That is, the branch only has flowing into it whatever is flowing in the vine because it is connected. Here is a question based on this truth: can sicknesses be found in the vine (Jesus Christ)? The answer is no, of course. So how can a branch that is connected to the vine have sicknesses flowing in it? Something must definitely be wrong somewhere.

Jesus lived on this same mosquito, virus, and bacteria-infested earth for over three decades and was never sick. What justification do you (as a branch) have to be sick? You need to know who you are and be conscious of your covenant rights in Christ Jesus so you don't live beneath your privileges. And even if you have been living beneath your privileges, you can become free if you are interested. Just get connected to the vine by covenant and stop tolerating anything you know cannot be found in Jesus.

Principle #7

The Bondage of Religion

John 8:31-36 KJV says *"Then said Jesus...If ye continue in my word, then are ye my disciples indeed; And ye shall know the truth, and the truth shall make you free. They answered him, We be Abraham's seed, and were never in bondage to any man: how sayest thou, Ye shall be made free?*

Jesus answered them, Verily, verily, I say unto you, Whosoever committeth sin is the servant of sin. And the servant abideth not in the house for ever: but the Son abideth ever. If the Son therefore shall make you free, ye shall be free indeed."

Religion doesn't guarantee liberation, only JESUS can set you free!

In religion, men device means by which they can relate with God (or god in some cases). They come up with certain practices that make them feel they are close to their deity. They follow all manners of rules just to get the approval of God or their god.

But Christianity is totally different. We don't look for God; He's the One looking for us (as lost sheep of His fold). He so much loves us that He can't just afford to lose us to the devil. Since the fall of man at the Garden of Eden, God had been making several efforts to get man back to Himself. He gave laws, sent judges, sent kings, and even sent prophets all to no avail because the issue of sin had not yet been settled. He then sent His only begotten Son –Jesus Christ – as the final blow to Satan and sin. Jesus did a very good job at the Cross of Calvary and reconciled the whole world back to the Father. As a result of this finished work of Christ, we no longer live by the law, keeping all manners of rules as if we are slaves. We have been adopted into the very family of God and we are now sons and daughters. Romans 8:15 NLT says *'So you have not received a spirit that makes you fearful slaves. Instead, you received God's Spirit when he adopted you as his own children. Now we call him, "Abba, Father."'*

We are no longer afraid of God's judgment because the full price for our sins has been paid. All we do now is fellowship with our Daddy in Heaven and simply carry out His will (instructions) here on earth.

If you want to be so busy in order to feel good or feel spiritual, then go for religion. Just know that no matter how good you feel in religion, you are still in bondage because no man can please God through self-righteousness or by keeping the laws. Romans 3:20-22 NIV says *'...no one will be declared righteous in God's sight by the works of the law; rather, through the law we become conscious of our sin. But now apart from the law the righteousness of God has been made known, to which the Law and the Prophets testify. This righteousness is given through faith in Jesus Christ to all who be-*

lieve...' And Isaiah 64:6 NLT says *'We are all infected and impure with sin. When we display our righteous deeds, they are nothing but filthy rags. Like autumn leaves, we wither and fall, and our sins sweep us away like the wind.'*

However, if you really desire a life of total freedom, you will need to invite Jesus into your life and let Him direct all your affairs. (John 8:32, 36). He is the ONLY ONE WHO CAN GIVE YOU THE TRUE MEANING OF FREEDOM.

Principle #8

Avoid the Sense Realm

2 Corinthians 10:3-6 KJV says *"For though we walk in the flesh, we do not war according to the flesh. For the weapons of our warfare are not carnal but mighty in God for pulling down strongholds, casting down arguments and every high thing that exalts itself against the knowledge of God, bringing every thought into captivity to the obedience of Christ, and being ready to punish all disobedience when your obedience is fulfilled."*

Never attempt to engage the devil in the sense realm – that is, in the natural realm.

In the realm of senses, Satan is a winner any day.

But in the realm of faith, he is a loser forever. If the devil can get you to focus on the things that are happening, he has captured you even though you may still be wearing good clothes and probably still speaking in tongues. The ONLY WAY to keep the devil in perpetual defeat is to keep dragging him to the faith region by simply telling him *'It is written'*.

But to achieve this, you will have to know what is written because he is smart enough to know what is and what is not written.

Did you remember the temptation of Jesus in the wilderness? That was a battle between what was happening and what is written. Let's read the account in Matthew 4:1-11 KJV *"Then was Jesus led up of the Spirit into the wilderness to be tempted of the devil. And when he had fasted forty days and forty nights, he was afterward an hungred. And when the tempter came to him, he said, If thou be the Son of God, command that these stones be made bread. But he answered and said, It is written, Man shall not live by bread alone, but by every word that proceedeth out of the mouth of God.*

Then the devil taketh him up into the holy city, and setteth him on a pinnacle of the temple, And saith unto him, If thou be the Son of God, cast thyself down: for it is written, He shall give his angels charge concerning thee: and in their hands they shall bear thee up, lest at any time thou dash thy foot against a stone. Jesus said unto him, It is written again, Thou shalt not tempt the Lord thy God.

Again, the devil taketh him up into an exceeding high mountain, and sheweth him all the kingdoms of the world, and the glory of them; And saith unto him, All these things will I give thee, if thou wilt fall down and worship me. Then saith Jesus unto him, Get thee hence, Satan: for it is written, Thou shalt worship the Lord thy God, and him only shalt thou serve. Then the devil leaveth him, and, behold, angels came and ministered unto him.'

Did you see how Jesus handled the temptation of the devil? The devil tried to drag Jesus to the sense realm by asking Him to convert stones to bread in order to satisfy His current need. But Jesus knew better; He dragged him back to the realm of faith by quoting the written Word of God to him, and eventually, that's what defeated him.

Don't be moved by what you see, what you hear or what you feel; rely totally on the Word of God. What is written will ALWAYS overcome what is happening.

So in summary, GRAB THE WORD OF GOD AND START USING IT, FOR THEREIN LIES YOUR VICTORY!

Principle #9

The ONLY Way

John 14:6 ESV says *"Jesus said to him, "I am the way, and the truth, and the life. No one comes to the Father except through me."*

Jesus is the ONLY WAY, not one of the ways!

Now when we talk about Jesus as the Way, what exactly does it mean? It means He is the only Way out of all unfavourable situations and the only Way into favourable situations.

There are several examples in the scripture to confirm this. We will look at some of them.

For instance, when Blind Bartimaeus met Jesus, he experienced Him as the Way in two dimensions.

Mark 10:46-52 NIV says *'Then they came to Jericho. As Jesus and his disciples, together with a large crowd, were leaving the city, a blind man, Bartimaeus (which means "son of Timaeus"), was sitting by the roadside begging. When he heard that it was Jesus of Nazareth, he began to shout, "Jesus, Son of David, have mercy on me!" Many rebuked him and told him to be quiet, but he shouted all the more, "Son of David, have mercy on me!" Jesus stopped and said, "Call him." So they called to the blind man, "Cheer up! On your feet! He's calling you." Throwing his cloak aside, he jumped to his feet and came to Jesus. "What do you want me to do for you?" Jesus asked him. The blind man said, "Rabbi, I want to see." "Go," said Jesus, "your faith has healed you." Immediately he received his sight and followed Jesus along the road.'*

According to this text, Blind Bartimaeus experienced Jesus as the Way out of his blindness (darkness) and the Way into his sight (light). The Way changed his life forever.

Also if you look at the story of the woman who

was caught in the act of adultery, she experienced Jesus as the Way too. John 8:3-11 NIV says *'The teachers of the law and the Pharisees brought in a woman caught in adultery. They made her stand before the group and said to Jesus, "Teacher, this woman was caught in the act of adultery. In the Law Moses commanded us to stone such women. Now what do you say?" They were using this question as a trap, in order to have a basis for accusing him. But Jesus bent down and started to write on the ground with his finger.*

When they kept on questioning him, he straightened up and said to them, "Let any one of you who is without sin be the first to throw a stone at her." Again he stooped down and wrote on the ground.

At this, those who heard began to go away one at a time, the older ones first, until only Jesus was left, with the woman still standing there. Jesus straightened up and asked her, "Woman, where are they? Has no one condemned you?" "No one, sir," she said. "Then neither do I condemn you," Jesus declared. "Go now and leave your life of sin."'

The law required that the woman should be

stoned to death for committing adultery. But upon coming face-to-face with Jesus, she experienced Him as her way out of death and her way into a new life.

I could go on and on. But the most important thing is this; you need to believe that the Lord Jesus is the Way, the Truth, and the Life according to John 14:6 before you can begin to enjoy Him as the way out of all your predicaments and the way into your much-desired life.

Jesus is the way out of chaos and the way into a lasting peace. In what way(s) do you want to experience the Way today? Go ahead and talk to Him in prayer.

Principle #10

All Power – Not Some

Matthew 28:18-20 KJV says *"And Jesus came and spake unto them, saying, All power is given unto me in heaven and in earth. Go ye therefore, and teach all nations, baptizing them in the name of the Father, and of the Son, and of the Holy Ghost: Teaching them to observe all things whatsoever I have commanded you: and, lo, I am with you alway, even unto the end of the world. Amen."*

And Psalm 62:11 KJV says *"God hath spoken once; twice have I heard this; that power belongeth unto God."*

All power still belongs to Jesus! Power to save,

the power to heal, the power to deliver, the power to set free, the power to make fruitful, the power to punish disobedience among others. All power belongs to Him.

Did you know that all principalities and powers are subject to Jesus? Read Colossians 1:15-16 in KJV; it says *'He is the image of the invisible God, the firstborn of all creation. For by Him all things were created, both in the heavens and on earth, visible and invisible, whether thrones or dominions or rulers or authorities—all things have been created through Him and for Him. He is before all things, and in Him all things hold together. He is also head of the body, the church; and He is the beginning, the firstborn from the dead, so that He Himself will come to have first place in everything. For it was the Father's good pleasure for all the fullness to dwell in Him,'*

You know what that means? It means those forces cannot carry out any operation unless Jesus (the Head) allows them. And that's why He said no weapon fashioned against you shall prosper (Isaiah 54:17).

The devil has no power, so don't attribute what is not his to him. If all power belongs to Jesus, then there is nothing left for the devil to claim. Your challenges cannot nullify this truth.

Receive divine intervention to ride above all storms of life in Jesus' Name.

Principle #11

He Loves You Notwithstanding

John 3:16-17 KJV says *"For God so loved the world, that he gave his only begotten Son, that whosoever believeth in him should not perish, but have everlasting life. For God sent not his Son into the world to condemn the world; but that the world through him might be saved."*

Beloved, Jesus really loves you. I mean even now that you are still stealing, telling lies, cheating, having premarital sex, addicted to alcohol and weed, etc. Even as you are bowing down to that moulded image in your room, He still loves you. You will NEVER come to understand the depth of His love for you until you accept His offer of salvation.

Romans 5:8 NLT says *'But God showed his great love for us by sending Christ to die for us while we were still sinners.'*

You see, God doesn't wait until we start behaving well before He shows us love. His love for us is not dependent on the number of things we do right. His love is not even dependent on our obedience to Him (even though His blessings depend on that), His love is simply based on Who He is. He is love Personified. 1 John 4:8 says God is love.

Look at the attitude of Jesus during His brutal crucifixion for instance; He wasn't angry with the people mocking and beating Him, rather, He prayed for them.

Luke 23:32-34 NIV says *'Two other men, both criminals, were also led out with him to be executed. When they came to the place called the Skull, they crucified him there, along with the criminals—one on his right, the other on his left. Jesus said, "Father, forgive them, for they do not know what they are doing." And they divided up his clothes by casting lots.'*

Even at death, He was still showing love. That's because His nature is love and no situation can change that.

However, the Lord doesn't just want to keep showering His love on you without you reciprocating it. He loves you and He wants you to love Him back. And to do that, you will have to hate what He hates and love what He loves. He hates sin and loves righteousness (Hebrew 1:9), therefore you too will have to hate sin by departing from it completely and love righteousness by embracing it fully.

So is there any sin in your life? Please go ahead and repent of it; then confess Jesus as your Lord and Saviour, you will be amazed at the outcome. He just wanted me to remind you of how much He loves you and I just did.

Principle #12

Peace by Knowledge

John 14:27 KJV says *"Peace I leave with you, my peace I give unto you: not as the world giveth, give I unto you. Let not your heart be troubled, neither let it be afraid."*

Maintaining an attitude of peace doesn't mean there are no troubles around, it only means your confidence in the Master of all storms is still intact. With Jesus in your boat, your journey is safe regardless of the stormy winds.

Ephesians 2:14 says Jesus Christ is our peace; so if you know Him, it means you know Peace. It is the knowledge of Jesus together with everything He is capable of doing that gives an assurance of peace when life seems to be going against us.

Jesus' disciples were traveling with Him at one time when suddenly a terrible storm arose. They were so perplexed that they thought they were actually perishing.

Let's read the story in Mark 4:35-41 NKJV: *'On the same day, when evening had come, He said to them, "Let us cross over to the other side." Now when they had left the multitude, they took Him along in the boat as He was. And other little boats were also with Him. And a great windstorm arose, and the waves beat into the boat, so that it was already filling. But He was in the stern, asleep on a pillow. And they awoke Him and said to Him, "Teacher, do You not care that we are perishing?"*

Then He arose and rebuked the wind, and said to the sea, "Peace, be still!" And the wind ceased and there was a great calm. But He said to them, "Why are you so fearful? How is it that you have no faith?" And they feared exceedingly, and said to one another, "Who can this be, that even the wind and the sea obey Him!"'

Could you imagine that as terrible as that storm was, Jesus was fast asleep? In fact, they needed to wake Him up because the storm just couldn't take away His sleep. And upon rising up, all He did was just to speak to the storm and that was the end. The storm vanished. How could Jesus sleep in such a life-threatening situation? Well, because one of His Names is 'The Prince of Peace' (Isaiah 9:6). He is Peace Himself. That's why in our opening text, He said 'My peace I give to you'. He is the Owner, that's why He could give it. And that tells us something straight away; without Jesus, there is no peace. In John 16:33 BSB, Jesus said *'I have told you these things so that in Me you may have peace. In the world you will have tribulation. But take courage; I have overcome the world!'"*

So are you really interested in enjoying lasting peace? Get connected to Jesus. He is the Only Licensed Distributor of Peace.

Principle #13

God will Make a Way

Exodus 14:15-31 KJV says *"And the LORD said unto Moses, Wherefore criest thou unto me? speak unto the children of Israel, that they go forward: But lift thou up thy rod, and stretch out thine hand over the sea, and divide it: and the children of Israel shall go on dry ground through the midst of the sea. And I, behold, I will harden the hearts of the Egyptians, and they shall follow them: and I will get me honour upon Pharaoh, and upon all his host, upon his chariots, and upon his horsemen. And the Egyptians shall know that I am the LORD, when I have gotten me honour upon Pharaoh, upon his chariots, and upon his horsemen.*

And the angel of God, which went before the camp of Israel, removed and went behind them; and the pillar of the cloud went from before their face, and stood behind them: And it came between the camp of the Egyptians and the camp of Israel; and it was a cloud and darkness to them, but it gave light by night to these: so that the one came not near the other all the night.

And Moses stretched out his hand over the sea; and the LORD caused the sea to go back by a strong east wind all that night, and made the sea dry land, and the waters were divided. And the children of Israel went into the midst of the sea upon the dry ground: and the waters were a wall unto them on their right hand, and on their left. And the Egyptians pursued, and went in after them to the midst of the sea, even all Pharaoh's horses, his chariots, and his horsemen. And it came to pass, that in the morning watch the LORD looked unto the host of the Egyptians through the pillar of fire and of the cloud, and troubled the host of the Egyptians, And took off their chariot wheels, that they drave them heavily: so that the Egyptians said, Let us flee from the face of Israel; for the LORD fighteth for them against the Egyptians.

And the LORD said unto Moses, Stretch out thine hand over the sea, that the waters may come again upon the Egyptians, upon their chariots, and upon their horsemen. And Moses stretched forth his hand over the sea, and the sea returned to his strength when the morning appeared; and the Egyptians fled against it; and the LORD overthrew the Egyptians in the midst of the sea. And the waters returned, and covered the chariots, and the horsemen, and all the host of Pharaoh that came into the sea after them; there remained not so much as one of them. But the children of Israel walked upon dry land in the midst of the sea; and the waters were a wall unto them on their right hand, and on their left.

Thus the LORD saved Israel that day out of the hand of the Egyptians; and Israel saw the Egyptians dead upon the sea shore. And Israel saw that great work which the LORD did upon the Egyptians: and the people feared the LORD, and believed the LORD, and his servant Moses."

God will make a way, even where there seems to be no way.

Nobody including Moses ever knew there was an expressway right in the midst of the Red Sea, but the Lord knew because He created the Red Sea. In the same way, you may not know how the Lord will solve your problems or deliver your expectations to you before the end of this year. But because He made a way for the Israelites where they didn't see any way before Pharaoh could catch up with them, He will make a way for you and your beautiful family before the year ends in Jesus' Name. To activate the fulfillment of your own, just say a believing 'Amen'.

Principle #14

Who Are Your Friends?

Mark 2:1-12 KJV says *"And again he entered into Capernaum, after some days; and it was noised that he was in the house. And straightway many were gathered together, insomuch that there was no room to receive them, no, not so much as about the door: and he preached the word unto them. And they come unto him, bringing one sick of the palsy, which was borne of four. And when they could not come nigh unto him for the press, they uncovered the roof where he was: and when they had broken it up, they let down the bed wherein the sick of the palsy lay.*

When Jesus saw their faith, he said unto the sick

of the palsy, Son, thy sins be forgiven thee. But there were certain of the scribes sitting there, and reasoning in their hearts, Why doth this man thus speak blasphemies? who can forgive sins but God only?

And immediately when Jesus perceived in his spirit that they so reasoned within themselves, he said unto them, Why reason ye these things in your hearts? Whether is it easier to say to the sick of the palsy, Thy sins be forgiven thee; or to say, Arise, and take up thy bed, and walk? But that ye may know that the Son of man hath power on earth to forgive sins, (he saith to the sick of the palsy,) I say unto thee, Arise, and take up thy bed, and go thy way into thine house.

And immediately he arose, took up the bed, and went forth before them all; insomuch that they were all amazed, and glorified God, saying, We never saw it on this fashion."

Look at what those four friends did in order to secure healing for their sick friend. They saw an opportunity for their friend's illness to end and they seized it, even when it meant tearing the roof of a house open in order to get him to Jesus. And did they get what they wanted? Sure, they did. Jesus saw their faith (expressed through their relentless efforts) and healed their friend.

Who are your friends? Are your friends drawing you to Jesus or drawing you away from Him? Do your friends tell you that you are taking this 'Jesus thing' too seriously? When you are in the company of your friends, do you feel close to God or you feel far away from Him?

You've got to choose your friends wisely and carefully. Any friend who doesn't feel comfortable with your relationship with Jesus Christ is likely going to draw you away from Him eventually.

Take a moment to reflect on your life and ask yourself this question: Which friends should I retain, and which ones should I release? Please don't be sentimental about this. Your sincere answer to this question will largely influence your life as you journey on. Say 'No' to friends who encourage you to smoke, drink, fornicate, fight, lie, owe and do things that are not honorable. Rather, choose friends like these four men in Mark 2:1-12 who carried their friend to Jesus and despite all obstacles ensured he got his healing. Any friend whose influence over your life tends towards you staying far from Jesus through sinful lifestyles must be avoided. This is very important especially at this time when eternity is fast approaching.

Remember, the Lord only commanded us to love everyone, He never commanded us to have relationship with everyone. May the wisdom to choose rightly come upon you in Jesus' Name.

Conclusion

So far, the Lord has revealed some biblical principles to us. The purpose is not just to know, document, or preach them, rather they were revealed so that we can walk in them.

According to John 8:32, only the truth that is known sets free. So, go through these principles one by one and determine to build your Christian walk around them for a life of Kingdom impact here on earth.

Jesus said in John 13:17(NLT) - *"You know these things- now do them! That is the path of blessing."*

May the Lord release upon you and your entire household the grace to walk worthy of His calling upon your lives in Jesus' Name!

WHY YOU REALLY NEED JESUS!

You might have heard a lot of Preachers talk about the importance of surrendering one's life to Jesus and even the dangers of not doing so at one time or the other without you being really moved. But with these three (3) important reasons highlighted below, I strongly believe you will not need another sermon before deciding to yield to His saving grace regardless of your religious beliefs.

1. **You have an Enemy to overcome:** There is an adversary who is all out to steal from you, kill you and destroy you regardless of your level of education, moral uprightness, societal influence or even religious beliefs. He is Devil by name (John 10:10, 1 Peter 5: 8), and he doesn't release any of

his captives until he completely destroys their souls in hell. The ONLY One Who can deliver you from his manipulations and also save your soul from him is Jesus Christ.

2. **You have an Appointment to keep:** Being alive and reading this implies you have a very important and inevitable appointment to keep. It is an appointment with death (Hebrews 9:27). Death is the sure end of all mortals (of which you are part); and to enable you prepare for this appointment without fear of eternal damnation, you need Jesus. He is the ONLY One Who has power over death (Revelation 1:18).

3. **You have a Judge to face:** Upon departure from this earth, you will have to stand before a judgment throne to render an account of your earthly life (Hebrews 9:27, Romans 14:12). The outcome of this judgment is what will determine your eternal abode which will either be Heaven

or the Lake of fire. Interestingly, the Judge Who will preside over your case and also decide where you will spend your eternity is Jesus (John 5:21-30, 2 Timothy 4:1). I perceive you are thinking "is God not our Judge? Why Jesus?' Well, you are not wrong. But God the Father Himself is the One Who handed over all the judgment to His Son, Jesus Christ. Read verse 22 of that John chapter 5. So Jesus is the ONLY One Who has the power to either judge you guilty or guiltless in eternity.

Now that you know these, the wisest thing you can do for yourself is to quickly establish a relationship with Jesus, since you don't even know how close your appointment with death is. To do this, say this prayer aloud:

"Lord Jesus, I am a sinner and I cannot help myself. Wash me in your precious blood and make me a new creature. I open the door of my heart to you today, come into my life, and become my Lord and Savior. Grant me the grace

to overcome the devil, prepare me for eternity, and help me to escape the judgment reserved for sinners. Thank You Jesus for saving me. Amen."

Congratulations! You are now SAVED. Go and sin no more.

To learn more about your new relationship with Jesus, kindly send an Email to info@gloem.org or emancipation4souls@yahoo.com, we will send you a material that will help you. You can also call, text, or send a WhatsApp message to +1 587 9735910 or +1 587 9695910 for further assistance.

And to learn more about God, His Word, and His plans for your life, kindly visit our Facebook page [*https://www.facebook.com/gloem.org*] for daily meditation in the Word of God (all year round) and our Blog page [*https://gloem.org/my-blog*] for life-transforming publications.

You are also invited to listen to Freedom Podcast: The Official Weekly Podcast of Global Emancipation Ministries – Calgary via https://anchor.fm/gloem

All these great resources capable of developing your spiritual stamina will help you become an overcomer in life regardless of what comes your way.

PRAYER POINTS

1. Father, thank You for opening my eyes to the truths contained in this book.
2. Father, please cause every experience in my life to work together for my good.
3. I cancel everything contrary to my prosperity and advancement in Jesus' Name.
4. God of all possibilities, please cause my grass to become green again.
5. From today, my breakthrough shall no longer be delayed in Jesus' Name.
6. Father, beginning from now, please release upon me and my household the ability to walk with you faithfully in the Name of Jesus.
7. Father, I thank You for answering all my prayers. Glory be to Your Holy Name. Hallelujah!

BECOME A FINANCIAL PARTNER WITH JESUS

At ***Global Emancipation Ministries - Calgary***, our mandate is ***to liberate men through the knowledge of the Truth*** and our mission statement is ***creating channels through which men can encounter the Truth - [Isaiah 61:1-3; John 8:32, 36; I Thessalonians 5:24].***

Our Ministerial Activities include Rural and Urban Evangelical Outreaches, Prison Evangelism, Hospital Ministrations, Mobilization for Missions Support, Teaching of the undiluted Word of God, Scripture-Based Seminars, Discipleship, Training of Field Missionaries and Empowerment of underprivileged ones among other Field Ministerial Tasks.

If you sense the Lord is calling you to reach out to the lost by engaging in any of these activities or by assisting those involved with your resources, please feel free to join us. Let us come together as we take the Gospel of our Lord Jesus Christ to the hurting and forgotten ones. [Mark 16:15-20].

Please join us in these kingdom projects by making your weekly, monthly, quarterly, or annual donations to Global Emancipation Ministries – Calgary.

You can visit the "GIVE" section on our website, www.gloem.org, to learn about the ways to give.

For acknowledgment, please advise your donations to us by email: info@gloem.org or emancipation4souls@yahoo.com, and kindly include your details i.e. name, address, email, and location. Alternatively, you can simply call +1 587 9735910 to do same.

You can also volunteer your gifts and talents

in the service of the Lord through our ministerial platforms regardless of your location. To get information on how to go about this, please visit www.gloem.org and contact us via email: info@gloem.org or emancipation4souls@yahoo.com.

God bless you.

About the Author

By the special grace of God, **Anthony O. Adefarakan** is the privileged President of **Global Emancipation Ministries - Calgary (GLOEM)** with headquarters in Canada, North America and **Emancipating Truth Ministry International (ETMI)** with headquarters in Nigeria, West Africa.

The Lord called him into the field ministry in February 2008 with the mandate to liberate men through the knowledge of the Truth, and by December 2012 he was ordained and commissioned as the Pioneer Pastor – in – Charge of The Redeemed Christian Church of God, Revelation Parish, Shalom Area under Delta Province III, Nigeria where he served until 1st February 2015 when he officially handed over to a new Pastor in order to focus on his field ministry to which the Lord had earlier called him and for which the authority of the church had already prayed and released him to undertake.

On 29th September 2013, he was awarded a Post Graduate Diploma in Tent – Making Mission from the Redeemed Christian School of Missions, Nigeria (RECSOM, Asaba Campus) where he also had the privilege to train Pastors and Missionaries as a lecturer in 2017.

Since the commissioning of his field ministry in 2015 he has had the opportunity to lead his ministry officers to field ministrations in different Prisons, Hospitals, Orphanages, Rural communities, Camp settlements, Markets, Local churches among other places with great successes on all occasions – such as salvation of sinners, healing of the sick, financial empowerment of mission churches, provision of relief materials to the poor, provision of medical services to the underprivileged, baptism in the Holy Ghost, deliverance from demonic oppression, release of inmates just to mention a few - all to the glory of God Who alone is the Doer.

He is the author of other best-selling titles such as *The Law of Kinds, Learning From the Ants, The Immutability of God's Counsel, Surely there is an End, Life Applicable lessons from the Book of Ruth, One thing is Needful Weekly Devotional Guide, Life Applicable Revelations from God's Word* (Volumes 1 and 2) among others.

He is blissfully married to Ifeoluwa A. Adefarakan and their marriage is fruitful to the glory of God.

Jesus is his Message, Freedom is the Outcome! Isaiah 61:1-3

www.ingramcontent.com/pod-product-compliance
Lightning Source LLC
Chambersburg PA
CBHW021430070526
44577CB00001B/151